Wendy DeGroat's *Beautiful Machinery* is a fine collection of intelligent, witty and moving poetry. She is direct without ever being simple. Her ear is excellent and she creates webs of sound. She writes love poems that are sensual and never sentimental. These poems bring you in contact with someone you want to know.
—Marge Piercy, award-winning author of a memoir, 17 novels, and 19 books of poetry, most recently *Made in Detroit*

Reading Wendy DeGroat's poetry makes me think of the phrase, "daily bread." Precise imagery, the joy of internal rhymes, and the light touch of formality are abundant in these poems. Attuned to the music of spoken word, DeGroat's lyricism and her sense of connection to the natural world, to the "beautiful machinery" of the beloved's body, provide substance and sustenance for the heart, for the imagination.
—Janice Gould, author of *Doubters and Dreamers,* and the forthcoming chapbook, *The Force of Gratitude*

The female body, that "beautiful machinery," is Wendy DeGroat's subject. It is the "lit wick flaring" or the tingle of taut nipples that makes it so "hard/to get ready for work." In language luscious and liquid, these poems invite the reader to join her in wonder and praise.
—Kim Roberts, Co-Editor, *Beltway Poetry Quarterly*

Wendy DeGroat's *Beautiful Machinery* draws its title from "Running Late," a playful and beautifully wrought poem about the body's wonders, yet the book maps not just the body. It expands to cover the difficult territory of marriage, divorce, sexuality, feminism, and new love—all with the same tender honesty of the title poem. In "Ode to Spiders" she writes, "Webs etch-a-sketched across the deck, / watch them cast lines, ride the wind." DeGroat has etch-a-sketched her own lines across traditional themes—and they merit your careful attention.
—Sierra Golden, author of *Aristotle's Lantern*

Beautiful Machinery

Beautiful Machinery

Wendy DeGroat

Headmistress Press

Copyright © 2016 by Wendy DeGroat
All rights reserved.

ISBN-13: 978-0997914979
ISBN-10: 0997914971

This book may not be reproduced, in whole or in part, including illustrations, in any form (beyond that permitted by Sections 107 and 108 of the U.S. Copyright Law and except by reviewers for the public press), without written permission from the publishers.

Cover art © 2015 by Jen P. Harris. *Ghost Study #5*. Ink on paper, 22 x 15 inches. Image courtesy of the artist.
Cover & book design by Mary Meriam.

PUBLISHER
Headmistress Press
60 Shipview Lane
Sequim, WA 98382
Telephone: 917-428-8312
Email: headmistresspress@gmail.com
Website: headmistresspress.blogspot.com

For Annette

Contents

Ride	1
Ode to Spiders	2
Fuel	3
Freight	4
Call and Response	5
No Way But Through	6
In nature journaling	7
Congregation	8
Listen	9
Negotiating Our First New Year's Eve	11
When I'm Asked, *Have You Ever Been Pregnant?*	12
Regeneration	13
The aphorist says	14
Marriage Spoon	15
Why the House Isn't Clean	16
Running Late	17
Heat Warning	18
When She Tells Me	19
Legally Equal	20
Gratefulness	22
Good Neighbors	23
Revenant	24
Preparing the Garden	25
Meditation on Time	26
Snowshoeing in the Park	27
If I Die First	28
About the Author	31
Acknowledgements	32
Poem Notes and Dedications	33
Gratitude	34

Ride

It beckoned from cellar shadows as we trundled past
on our down-bundled tumble into the pickup truck
or zipped by close enough to clip its waiting flanks
on our race to retrieve a jar of peaches or pickles.

It hung from a rope slung over a ceiling truss,
red lumber dulled by dust, worn to a rust hue
by years of Zorro and the Lone Ranger:
horse swing we rode to the dryer's rumble,

rode to the washer's squeak and swish, rode
as if a posse stampeded toward us through thunder
and driving rain, garage scents of oil and metal
like gunsmoke's sting in our nose and eyes,

blue-jeaned thighs gripping the seat, sneakered feet
thrusting our steed faster, strained rope creaking
like saddle leather, one hand feathering the reins,
other arm raised in the wind rushing across the plains.

Ode to Spiders

They are among the first wonders I discover.
Along with clouds, yeast rolls doubling
on the counter, and a brother who grows
in Mom's belly, they mesmerize me
long before I hear of the man in spandex
who claims their name. Mornings, I find
webs etch-a-sketched across the deck,
watch them cast lines, ride the wind.

I've studied them since. Learned those silk spouts
are spinnerets. But what stuns me is spider sex.
As in humans, their males produce sperm, but
they don't fertilize a female's eggs. She does.
Instead, he deposits his offering in a pocket
of hers, and she holds it there until she's ready.
As if a woman could say to a man, leave that
on the counter. I'll decide when to use it. If.

Fuel

Every time I smell gasoline, I see her again.

Top down on her low-slung convertible,
Texaco star overhead, she
unfolds from the driver's seat,
        easing to the pump in one slow long-legged glide.

I drag my gaze back
to the numbers' predictable grids, clench
the pump's trigger against my ring,
concentrate on looking straight
ahead, but at the edge of my vision
                      her figure shimmers.

Last tug toward .00	spills from the tank.
Pump clicks off.	Mind stays on—her.
I train my stare on	oil stains,
reread the warning	about sparks.
Did I just imagine	kissing her, sliding my palms along her thighs?

I don't even know her.

As my fingers linger over the ignition,	the something that threatens to take down the past decade: husband, friendships, family— sears through me.

    I take a long sip   of the view   in my rear-view

    and pull

away.

Freight

I will leave him.
In a house where we lounged on sun-washed Sundays,
laughed, dreamt, his hand cupped
over my belly's empty home, I will leave him.

In our living room, it will happen like this: my coming out
like the night sky tearing, and when I reach for him
across the shredded air, he will turn away,
shout for me to go, and I will leave.

I will leave him. Leave the house, our bed, the rocking
chair, his yell coupling his pain to my body so that each time
I hear freight cars collide and moan in the train yard,
that night and its broken pieces pierce my belly.

It will happen like this. I will tell him. I will
hurt him. He will tell me to leave, and I will.

Call and Response

Gossip rises from the tall grass,
dry din joining
leaf-rattle,
birdsong,
wind's rush
        across the ears' open bowls:

summer hymn.

The earth inhales,
        stillness—
            then begins the next verse:
        grass-gossip
     wasp-whisper
hawk cry.

No Way But Through

In the moment I learn of my power
to inflict pain, as my words cut him rough
as any blunt blade, I want to forget this agony
was a cost I understood before I spoke.

So that days later across the kitchen table
I offer him anything. As if a rocking chair
or house is enough to close the gash,
erase the choice of my survival over his.

Our marriage a mountain then,
my future an interstate pushing through it,
my decision the dynamite's blast
from which some stones would not be recovered.

Now through the lens of decades I know
he thrives—a better job, another wife, the children
I did not have. And I do too. Work that feeds me.
A beloved who ignites my desire and drive.

But this resilience is nothing I could know then.
I only knew where I'd stand after
was a place I couldn't reach otherwise,
no matter how long I kept climbing.

In nature journaling

it is in the third act of looking that we begin to see
more clearly, the instructor says.

When I sketch a tree peony, it is the tight bud on the bush
I see first, then rain lingering on the leaves like moonstones

adorning so many outstretched hands. Third time I notice
how freckles speckle the bud, crimson veins stripe the stems,

the way branches undulate in the breeze,
raised arms swaying in wordless praise.

So it is with you.

When I glance up from the hymnal, I see you
standing before the congregation, firm, then watch

as your gaze sweeps across our faces like sunlight spreading
along dune grass. Later, as I wait for a friend to introduce us,

my cheeks warm, I notice how you are planted, stance steady,
wide, see those copper highlights in your hair as you

lift your hand toward mine.

Congregation

After weeks of gray damp, we emerge on a January Sunday, converging on the park, with dogs and without, with children and without, with—or by ourselves. Here. Cyclists in matching jerseys pedal in sync. Grinning tall on her princess bike, a girl careens toward her dad's camera. Beneath a willow, two women whisper, hold hands. Henry, who lives under the overpass, who warns folks, *slow down, take it easy,* he's out too. Frisbee-golfers stride uphill. A boy skates downhill. Little sister chases him, squealing. Runners, fingers pressed to pulse, count the seconds. Beside the spillway, an old man lounges, pole in hand. And sunset men, in the lot where they've found and lost each other for decades, lean soft on dark-windowed cars. As tree shadows flicker, merge, my lungs lift like birds from a cage flung open.

>   Voices and sunlight caught
>   in winter grass
>   beside the water's rush.

Listen

If you haven't stepped onto a street and looked
both ways not for traffic but for who
might cram a rag down your throat, ram the
opening between your thighs with the could-be
billy-club part of him he packs each day,

how could you know.

If you haven't measured an alley, driveway,
or gravel road for how long it would take to cross,
how long to get from where you are
to safety, calculated the odds, knowing strangers' fists
loom stronger than yours, that anything you carry
might be used against you, and the road is slick,

how could you know.

And even though when it almost happened,
you escaped with cut cheek and asphalt eye,
even on days you pull on boots or power suit, arm yourself
with knife or phone or fifteen affirmations of your blessings,
it doesn't stop fear, at a footstep's crunch, from dragging the
breath from your throat, swelling like floodwater
inside your chest, insistent, deafening—and you picture women,
men and women banging pots in Chile and South Africa
to sound the alarm of a beating, or the ones in India ringing
bells, and you stretch your eyes and ears wide, searching
for who might hear your scream, and bang, bang, bang.

Tell me, you say, *tell me,* and that's what I'm doing now,
but even if you lean in, hold me, listen close, what you're learning
is about me, about then, not what it's like to be me. And me, who've
never cradled a fevered child at four a.m., praying the ice bath
will work because there's nothing left for a doctor or food—

how can I know, even if I lean toward her, listen close.

Our dark alleys, the way fear or mercury rises, the reasons we pray
or give up on God, the clanging inside, the way we yearn
for someone to carry our story's echo in their bones—even if it's
not the same as living in each other's skin, if we don't invite
each other in, say *tell me,* sit quiet and still, say again, *tell me,* and wait

how will we know.

Negotiating Our First New Year's Eve

> *We live in the illusion of beginnings and endings*
> – Jennifer Sweeney

After Christmas, delivery men arrive, ask, *where do you want 'em?*
about the couch, love seat, and recliner we selected weeks before.

You are not here, driving instead into a turnpike storm near Boston,
snow falling like shredded clouds onto your windshield.

Here, and here, I point as the men tear off plastic, move pieces
into place—our first purchase together, another beginning.

You attend another ending. Former lover dying, cancer returning
to her body after five years offshore—to make its harbor there.

New Year's Eve, mirrored ball descends to a rising chant
while you watch her breathe. Cameras zoom in on couples kissing

in Times Square, confetti caught in their hair.
On our couch, I imagine you beside me,

hear you remind me love is not a finite thing, there is enough
for her and me. *Enough*—I toast to your love for both of us.

When I'm Asked, *Have You Ever Been Pregnant?*

I see myself in the high school cafeteria, leaning in to hear
above the clamor. In stirrup pants, leg warmers, I'm a confusion
of books, boyfriends, backpack tiled with buttons: *Cats, Not Kids.*

After college, a decade passes with a husband. Cats. No attempts
to make it otherwise. Then that afternoon in a friend's kitchen—
my arm stretched to spread paint, I feel the air behind me ignite.

                                              When I let go
of the roller, turn, I am pressed between sheetrock
and a woman's weight. Around me, everything tinder.

Yet most times, a later scene lingers: calendars, my feet in stirrups,
injections. Then cramps. Embrace of a woman who loved me then.
Scene repeated again and again. Fruitless pursuit for what my body
      would not bear.

Regeneration

When I met her I wasn't thinking about forever
or even fall, imprints from the last leaving

so fresh I didn't even know
if I wanted something new.

Then, amid a March game's din, her thumb
traveled my palm—singing stick circling

a meditation bowl's rim. *De-
fense,* the crowd chanted. I let her in.

After the game, nearby park, my shoulders
pressed against bark, her mouth hovered

over mine, gaze savoring me the way
a wine taster swirls merlot on the tongue.

Months later, midmorning, branches dance
on the walls; scent, like a forest after rain,

rises in the room. I lift my lips from hers,
absorb the yes shining from her eyes.

Loved. I've been that before, but not this
too: wanted, and the wanting back,

a seedling pushing through ash. This
is what it feels like to be beautiful.

The aphorist says

when shown two shapes:
one jagged, one round,

and asked which is called
bouba, which kiki,

we match name to shape
by sound, proof

synesthesia is something
we all carry around.

Arriving home low, I go outside.
Four swallowtails lilt by.

I'm mesmerized, nestle
deep in my chair. As I tilt

my face toward fading blue,
a chickadee plucks the air.

Then, just as I give thanks
for this day and wings' grace,

a jay drops to the feeder,
a heavy bass.

There are a thousand notes to be flown,
a thousand ways to praise.

Marriage Spoon

Our friend has carved two maple leaves touching
to form a handle, then shaped the whorled bowl long
and deep, like a thumbprint pressed in the tree's rings.
"Canadian," he says, placing it in our hands unwrapped,
spoon and his maple lapel pin tangible as we embrace.

Canada. That escape each of us considered
when candidates stumped against our love
and votes to let it take root in our country failed.
       We remained planted.
Couldn't this be the journey of any union?

Releasing from the veined block with which we begin
the form within, shaping from separate leaves
something we can hold, and in those moments we
sense the urge for flight in our branches, coaxing it
instead to sing into the deep bowl of morning.

Why the House Isn't Clean

I swear, when I woke, I was intent on it.
It was on my list. Then gray skies, rain,

so little light to clean by. Newspapers
piled by the window. Isn't sorting

a kind of cleaning? Hours later, clippings
in tidy stacks. Then the sun came out.

Perfect time for errands. And on the drive home,
a poem. I muted the radio, ignored roadside lilies,

rain-slick and open, their call. Lines
blossomed. I struggled to hold them all.

Home, I raced down the hall, past vacuum,
mop. When fingers stalled on keys,

I pondered what to cook. What will you
crave? You've been away so long.

Then your key in the door. I rush to greet you,
almost apologizing for a mess I'm not sorry for.

Between kisses, you brim with talk of lilies, rain,
drop your bags on the floor—say nothing

of dusting left undone. As I reach to sweep
mail from the table, you pull me into the sun.

Running Late

Sometimes a body makes it hard
to get ready for work. Take nipples,
for instance. The way, when kissed
by a cold draft after a shower, they rise up
like a kid in the front row of class
waving both hands. You see them—
and you just have to stand there and gaze,
amazed by the way blood rushes,
plumps them to tight berries,
how the tingle jingles through your body.

While you should be making coffee,
packing lunch, you remember how,
in a crowded room, they perk up
near the one with promising lips
and sure hips, twin pulse pulling you
toward *hello*. This magic—
the magic of our bodies' beautiful machinery,
if I were to show you what I know so far
about the Holy, I'd begin with this.

Heat Warning

Thankless August, heat that slicks flesh steam-wet
in seconds as my legs crank to crest the hill,
muscles clenching with each push-pull on the pedals,
physical presence supplanting thought with body, body,
body—lit wick flaring toward others of my species.
Bronze men swarm a soccer ball, and longing
hums through my thighs. Then, along the road's curve,
a runner emerges, phone pressed to her lips—the urge
to coax the cell from her grip, to sink beside her
in the scrubgrass between treeline and chainlink,
nearly succumbs, something elemental surging from calf
to wrist, sweat the only pressure valve against burning.
I return home, pulse pounding, quads tense.
Darling, singe me to breath.

When She Tells Me

This is when she doesn't.

Not while I sprinkle cayenne onto the chick peas
as she bubbles over about goldfinch at the feeder,

Not as the sun slants onto the coffee table
and she hits play on the DVR, iPads in our laps,

Not before her evening bath. Not even when she comes
to bed as I vie to stay awake for one more page.

No. Instead, it is minutes before midnight. Thursday.
I lean into her, drift toward sleep, her skin fragrant, warm.

But then like those mornings when the garbage truck
blocks the driveway just as I'm backing out for work,

she tells me how disappointed she was on Tuesday
when I said I'd read her latest draft this weekend.

When I offer to read it tomorrow, that's wrong
too. How can I be not fast enough—and too soon?

I sit up, thumbs crunched white against the page. She turns
to her screen, fist pulsing on the sheet between us.

Cicada-cries rise through the closed window. Years ago,
solo again but stubbornly hopeful, I prayed for a woman

who believes change is possible, works for justice, wants it—
now. This urgency comes with the answering. Slow

breath fills my belly, lungs. Above the cicadas' thrum,
she wishes aloud that she'd waited to tell me. I vow

to read her story in the morning. Her hand opens.

Legally Equal

> *October 6, 2014, was the first day same-sex couples could legally marry in Virginia.*

= *LOVE*. It's engraved inside our wedding bands,
what we believe but didn't believe would be legal here

in our lifetime. Then news broke the Supreme Court
refused to hear appeals of rulings that allowed us

to tie the knot. How I heard, where, in whose voice,
a fork the rest of my days will be tuned by:

my beloved telling me the news with a question,
"Do you want to get married in the morning?" *Yes. Oh*

my God. I don't remember which I said first.
I didn't expect it would feel this different.

Years ago, we signed papers for the almost-wed
we could approximate. Now, in our Southern state,

parents adopt children they've raised for more than a decade,
couples add each other to insurance policies,

and the two of us, under stars and stripes outside the courthouse,
clutch our marriage license, testing its weight and wings—

every Facebook post, call, full of awe for each possible thing.
Then friends share their story about that first night

the equality we'd imagined came true. As they hurried
to a party, holding hands, already giddy, one whispered,

her eyes scanning the sidewalk, shadows, faces,
Honey, let's not stay out too late, someone might beat us up.

Her lover hugged her, then tugged her inside their favorite diner
where they toasted the day and whispered prayers for the days after.

Gratefulness

Steamed artichokes with butter, the vibration of an incoming text,
muddy boots, summits, parking lot kisses, a loon's sunset call,
wholeness, fireflies, lilacs, moonlight after rain, another
chance, bird feeder rush hour, the cursor's steady pulse,
grace before meals, our favorite ginger cookies, both cars
in the driveway, the sacramental slide of skin against skin,
October, gathered friends, meandering conversations, less fear
of dying, a guitar's strum, the blessing of falling asleep in her arms.

Good Neighbors

They're the people you talk to while leaning on the fence,
hair mussed, still in your pajamas, the ones who plant lilies
and roses, who let squirrels nest in their soffit through winter
then delight when the babies chase each other along the roof,
whose laughter when they're gathered out back drifts in your windows,
whose morning exchanges with their dogs mark the start of most days,
whose burgers grilling make your mouth water, who invite you
to supper, the ones you share your favorite stout with, those bottles
you waited in line for, who hire a neighbor in need of work for chores
they could do themselves, who borrow tools and return them.
They are people the world needs more of.

Revenant

For the first time in years, it happens again—
those menacing shouts at held hands.
"Fuckin' dykes!" men snarl from a truck window,
tires crunching grit along the curb as they slow,
hurled words landing like fists,
rape the fix they threaten next.
If there were a court for this, they'd say we asked for it.

They gun the engine, gone before we turn.
But they've already brought you back—
dear, fierce woman
who once stopped another woman's knuckles
from busting my lip, pinned her anger down
in a narrow hallway—your strength, will,
leaving her only curses and spit to hit with.

You loved like that too. Brother, nephew, students,
me. Your love for us larger than the narrow places
alcohol or hate had brought you face-to-face
with love's limits. I remember how you held my gaze,
your eyes a calm horizon above that woman's storm,
how you restrained her until her fury ebbed,
then let her go, none of us bloody or bruised.

I wonder who you're protecting now.

Preparing the Garden

There is satisfaction in the reclaiming,
defining again where things end and begin.
Twigs and leaf-debris cleared from beds.
Dime-high seedlings, oak and holly, pulled,
weeds too. Willow fence restaked. Bench
brushed clean. Afterward, shoulders
and back that good kind of weary. Heat
seeps from my t-shirt as I rest in the shade,
peaceful riot of birdsong and traffic, cheers
from a distant ballgame, a fountain gurgling.

    What more could I wish of this place?

As I think this, two sparrows race past.
And for the first time as my eyes follow
their flight, I notice a Celtic cross
under the neighbors' Nandina and recall
the dogs they lost this winter and our cat
we lost this fall. I wonder if the cross
marks one or both their losses or whether
it's planted to help us remember them all.

Meditation on Time

> *Everyone forgets that Icarus also flew.*
> – Jack Gilbert

Five years was what I asked for,
belovéd born fourteen years before me.

I made a pledge.
Give us five years of this love, Universe,

and whatever comes after,
I won't complain.

I imagined a quiet current carrying us.
But it was floodwater quick.

When we reached the shore I'd bargained for,
two prayers: Thank you. More.

Joy, some say, is the hardest feeling
to abide, fear of its balloon breaking

keeping its string in our fist
even as it tugs toward sky.

When this joy ends,
when the joy that lifts me now

is torn open by sorrow's cry,
don't stop my tears—

remind me what it felt like to fly.

Snowshoeing in the Park

I imagine another time
        whalebone and sinew
                blank expanses on folded maps.

Trees bend toward me, listening,
        snowshoed steps like branches
                creaking, a path of cracked snow circles,

the way thrown stones disrupt water.
        Ahead deer tracks and squirrel prints,
                bird scratch against the thicket's edge.

As the snow holds under my weight,
        I stand closer to the burnished sky.
                A hawk's cry pierces the low hush

of wind and stream.
        Rust-breasted sentinel,
                he watches me from an oak's

highest perch before launching
        from woodline to field, his call
                all hunt and hunger—what persists

across time and season
        what got us here
                what pulls us on.

If I Die First

After the burning's done, pour
what's left in a Mason jar—nothing new,

but one washed clean of applesauce or pickled beets,
the clear kind that kids keep fireflies inside.

Let my cinders rest there
like sand art in jelly jars carried home from the fair.

If the small or gray of me unsettles you,
pin flannel or fleece around the glass,

leaving a gap, thumb-wide, under the rim, enough
to let sun and moonlight in. Store me beside the poetry.

When it feels right, talk to me, sing, or sit by quietly.
For a wheel of seasons, take me down. Hold me open—

to campfires, fallen leaves, a lilac's laden bough.
Press me deep in moss and snow.

When my birthday comes, add a pinch of salt,
toast to us with good bourbon or dark rum.

And when you're ready to move on, release me somewhere
we once were. As dust blurs through your fingers,

quick or slow, know I miss your touch, and let me go.

Photo of Wendy DeGroat by Georgianne Stinnett, 2016

About the Author

Wendy DeGroat's poetry has appeared in U.S. and U.K. publications, including those in the acknowledgements, as well as *About Place, Common-place, Forage, Rogue Agent Journal,* and *The Brillantina Project*. With degrees in English literature, education, and library studies, her research interests include 19th and 20th century women's history, especially working women and women who founded and led schools. She's currently writing documentary poetry about two such women who had a lasting impact on Richmond, Virginia: Grace Evelyn Arents and Mary Garland Smith.

Wendy grew up in the Appalachian foothills of northern New Jersey and western Virginia, and now lives in Richmond, where she works as a librarian, teaches writing workshops, and curates poetryriver.org, a resource site for documentary poetry and for diversifying the poetry taught in high school and undergraduate classrooms. She also advocates for human equality, including serving as a small-group facilitator for Living the Richmond Pledge, a workshop that empowers participants to take leadership in ending racism in their communities and in our culture. *Beautiful Machinery* is her first book.

Acknowledgements

Warmest thanks to the editors and readers of the publications in which these poems first appeared or will appear soon, sometimes in slightly different forms:

Algebra of Owls: "When I'm Asked, Have You Ever Been Pregnant?" and "Preparing the Garden"

Beltway Poetry Quarterly: "Freight," "In nature journaling," and "When She Tells Me"

Mslexia: "Ode to Spiders"

Raleigh Review: "Running Late"

Rust + Moth: "If I Die First"

Silver Birch Press *My Prized Possession* series: "Marriage Spoon"

Sprout: "Gratefulness"

The Dead Mule School of Southern Literature: "Congregation"

TRIVIA: Voices of Feminism: "Listen"

"When I'm Asked, *Have You Ever Been Pregnant?*" won the October 2016 Readers' Choice Award for *Algebra of Owls*.

Poem Notes and Dedications

"Ride" to my parents.

"Marriage Spoon" to Norm Craig.

"Legally Equal" to Rev. Jeanne Pupke, Rev. Dr. Hope Johnson, Charlotte Davenport, Dr. Janice Marie Johnson, Rev. Nan White, Rev. Joy Christi Przestwor, Chris Mohn, Sally Wetzler, and everyone who attended our wedding celebration or the brief 2014 ceremony that made our marriage legal, as well as every person who worked to make marriage equality a reality, including Edie Windsor, Carol Schall and Mary Townley, Timothy Bostic and Tony London, and all the plaintiffs in *Obergefell v. Hodges*.

"Gratefulness" – after Dan Albergotti's "Among the Things He Does Not Deserve."

"Good Neighbors" to Christine Maggard and Brooke Rogers.

Gratitude

Gratitude to Jeanne Hildebrand, teacher and friend, who helped me discover the art and joy of poetry in high school when I was still forming the first draft of myself, to Dr. Paul D'Andrea, who taught me to draw inspiration from many sources, to Laure-Anne Bosselaar, a gifted poet whose patient mentoring has guided me to improve my craft and take more risks in my writing, and to Marge Piercy, whose poetry motivated me to write about difficult and beautiful things, and whose intensive poetry workshop introduced me to a talented and supportive community of poets.

Thank you to friends who read early drafts of my poems, especially Joy Przestwor, Charlotte Davenport, Chris Mohn, Jeanne Pupke, and Regina Largent, and more family and friends who encourage me to keep writing like my parents, Aunt Dee, Aunt Tillie, Aunt Bell, Page Brannon, Janice Marie Johnson, Hope Johnson, Cindy Cain, Anne Walpole, Bonnie Nemeth, Gahan Kelley, Nan White, Sam Ballenger, and Charlotte Cowtan, as well as writers in my workshops around RVA and in James River Writers. Thank you also to my colleagues who read or write poetry, or who invite contemporary poetry into their classrooms, including into unexpected places like Military History.

Jubilant gratitude to Headmistress Press for selecting this manuscript for an Editors' Choice Award, to Mary Meriam for her vision and talent in designing this book, and to Jen P. Harris, who granted permission for "Ghost Study #5" to be used in the cover design. This piece is part of *Ghost Prairie*, a large-scale installation that "evokes the simultaneous presence and absence" of the Iowa prairie. Each tile can only be fully seen by the viewer if they step close. May this stunning art beckon readers to step close to this book, and in turn, to explore more of Jen P. Harris's work (jenpharris.com)

In this ancestry of words and humanity, thank you also to Anne-Marie Oomen, Staceyann Chin, Nikky Finney, Ellen Bass, Lucille Clifton, Aracelis Girmay, Richard Blanco, Patricia Smith, Matthew Olzmann, Dorianne Laux, Jericho Brown, Adrienne Rich, Claudia Rankine,

Shailja Patel, Ross Gay, Aimee Nezhukumatathil, Naomi Shihab Nye, Martín Espada, Andrea Gibson, and Mark Doty, some of the dazzling writers whose work has shown me how to intertwine and celebrate our multi-faceted human experience in poetry. Among those facets for me: woman, daughter, lover, wife, lesbian, feminist, citizen, teacher, and spinning cog within this wondrous mystery that embraces us all.

Deepest gratefulness to my parents, whose love gave me wings and continues to uplift me, and to my wife, Annette Marquis, who is my writing companion and first reader, and whose joyous, playful, generous love is a blessing for which I give thanks each day.

Headmistress Press Books

Odd Mercy - Gail Thomas

The Great Scissor Hunt - Jessica K. Hylton

A Bracelet of Honeybees - Lynn Strongin

Whirlwind @ Lesbos - Risa Denenberg

The Body's Alphabet - Ann Tweedy

First name Barbie last name Doll - Maureen Bocka

Heaven to Me - Abe Louise Young

Sticky - Carter Steinmann

Tiger Laughs When You Push - Ruth Lehrer

Night Ringing - Laura Foley

Paper Cranes - Dinah Dietrich

A Crown of Violets - Renée Vivien tr. Samantha Pious

On Loving a Saudi Girl - Carina Yun

The Burn Poems - Lynn Strongin

I Carry My Mother - Lesléa Newman

Distant Music - Joan Annsfire

The Awful Suicidal Swans - Flower Conroy

Joy Street - Laura Foley

Chiaroscuro Kisses - G.L. Morrison

The Lillian Trilogy - Mary Meriam

Lady of the Moon - Amy Lowell, Lillian Faderman, Mary Meriam

Irresistible Sonnets - ed. Mary Meriam

www.ingramcontent.com/pod-product-compliance
Lightning Source LLC
Chambersburg PA
CBHW070040070426
42449CB00012BA/3112